Dear Dad, I Made This Book Just For You

Want a freebie?
Email us at

Benzerpress@gmail.com

Title the email «Story!» and
we'll send you something fun

THROUGHOUT THE BOOK
YOU WILL FIND
BLACK PAGES SIMILAR TO
THIS ONE
THESE ARE MEANT TO
PREVENT COLOR SEEPAGE
TO THE NEXT PAGES

YOU MAKE ME HAPPY WHEN

_____

_____

_____

_____

I LOVE IT WHEN YOU

YOU ARE GREAT AT

_____

_____

_____

MY FRIENDS TELL ME YOU ARE

YOU MAKE ME LAUGH WHEN

A 703R

YOU MAKE THE BEST

_____

_____

_____

_____

I LOVE TO GO WITH YOU TO

Let' go

I LOVE YOU MORE THAN

THE BEST MEMORY I HAVE OF YOU IS

YOU ARE MY SUPERHERO BECAUSE

_____

_____

I LOVE WHEN YOU TEACH ME

_____

_____

_____

_____

I LOVE YOU BECAUSE YOU GIVE ME A LOT OF

_____

_____

_____

_____

YOU ARE THE BEST AT

I LOVE WHEN WE PLAY

_____

_____

_____

MY WISH IS TO

_____

_____

_____

_____

I LIKE IT WHEN WE

MY FAVORITE THING TO DO
WITH YOU IS

_____

_____

I KNOW YOU WILL NEVER

_____

_____

_____

_____

I ALWAYS SMILE WHEN YOU

I WANT TO GO WITH YOU TO

Made in United States
North Haven, CT
07 June 2022